Charities as Beneficiaries

THIRD EDITION

Other titles available from Law Society Publishing:

Elderly Client Handbook (4th edn)
Caroline Bielanska and Martin Terrell (eds)

Lasting Powers of Attorney (2nd edn)
Craig Ward

Mental Capacity: A guide to the new law (2nd edn)
Nicola Greaney, Fenella Morris and Beverley Taylor

Probate Practitioner's Handbook (6th edn)
Lesley King (ed)

Trust Practitioner's Handbook (3rd edn) (forthcoming, 2012)
Gill Steel

Will Draftsman's Handbook (9th edn) (forthcoming, 2012)
Lesley King, Peter Gausden and Robin Riddett

Titles from Law Society Publishing can be ordered from all good bookshops or direct (telephone 0870 850 1422, email **lawsociety@prolog.uk.com** or visit our online shop at **www.lawsociety.org.uk/bookshop**).

Charities as Beneficiaries

THIRD EDITION

Law Society's Private Client Section
and the Institute of Legacy Management

All rights reserved. No part of this publication may be reproduced in any material form, whether by photocopying, scanning, downloading onto computer or otherwise without the written permission of the Law Society except in accordance with the provisions of the Copyright, Designs and Patents Act 1988. Applications should be addressed in the first instance, in writing, to Law Society Publishing. Any unauthorised or restricted act in relation to this publication may result in civil proceedings and/or criminal prosecution.

Whilst all reasonable care has been taken in the preparation of this publication, neither the publisher nor the authors can accept any responsibility for any loss occasioned to any person acting or refraining from action as a result of relying upon its contents.

The views expressed in this publication should be taken as those of the contributors only unless it is specifically indicated that the Law Society has given its endorsement.

© The Law Society 2012

Appendix A © Association of Contentious Trust and Probate Specialists
Appendix C © Smee & Ford Ltd
Appendix D © Institute of Legacy Management
Appendix F © Society of Trust and Estate Practitioners

ISBN-13: 978-1-907698-55-2

First edition 2003
Second edition 2008
This third edition published in 2012 by the Law Society
113 Chancery Lane, London WC2A 1PL

Typeset by Columns Design XML Ltd, Reading
Printed by TJ International Ltd, Padstow, Cornwall

The paper used for the text pages of this book is FSC® certified. FSC (the Forest Stewardship Council®) is an international network to promote responsible management of the world's forests.

Contents

About the contributors	ix
Preface	x
Introduction	xi

1 Drawing up wills — 1

- **1.1 Introduction** — 1
- **1.2 Identifying a charity correctly** — 1
  - 1.2.1 Verifying the name of the intended charity beneficiary — 1
  - 1.2.2 Bequests to local branches or committees — 1
  - 1.2.3 Specifying a particular project or purpose — 2
  - 1.2.4 Cy-près — 2
  - 1.2.5 Merged charities — 3
  - 1.2.6 Is the organisation a charity? — 3
- **1.3 Charity will-making schemes** — 4
  - 1.3.1 Will Aid — 4
  - 1.3.2 Remember a Charity — 4
  - 1.3.3 Charities paying for wills — 4
- **1.4 Managing risk** — 5
  - 1.4.1 Avoiding claims post-death — 5
  - 1.4.2 *Larke* v. *Nugus* statements — 6
  - 1.4.3 File retention and storage of the will — 6
  - 1.4.4 Validity of wills in suspicious circumstances — 6
- **1.5 Charities and tax planning** — 7
  - 1.5.1 Inheritance Tax (IHT) — 7
  - 1.5.2 Foreign charities — 7
- **1.6 Charities as executors** — 7
- **1.7 Application of funds left to charity** — 8
  - 1.7.1 Trusts for those with special needs — 8
  - 1.7.2 Bequests to branches of national charities — 8

	1.8	Alternative ways to benefit charities	9
	1.9	Executors' costs and expenses	9
	1.10	Statutory will applications	10

2 Administration of estates — 11

	2.1	Notification of benefit	11
		2.1.1 Communicating with charity beneficiaries	11
		2.1.2 Smee & Ford notification	11
	2.2	Terms and conditions letters	12
	2.3	The Royal Sign Manual procedure	12
	2.4	Rights of charity beneficiaries to information	12
		2.4.1 Pecuniary legacies	13
		2.4.2 Specific legacies	13
		2.4.3 Residuary legacies	14
	2.5	Common themes where charities are residuary beneficiaries	15
		2.5.1 Consulting charities before agreeing the sale of estate assets	15
		2.5.2 Liaising with a number of charities	15
		2.5.3 Transferring assets *in specie*	15
		2.5.4 Chattels requested by family or friends	16
	2.6	Estate accounts	16
		2.6.1 Legacy professionals' queries	16
		2.6.2 Fees	16
		2.6.3 Executors' expenses	17
		2.6.4 IHT and its apportionment	17
		2.6.5 Indemnities	18
	2.7	Claims against estates in which charities share residue	18
		2.7.1 Ex gratia claims	18
		2.7.2 Charity procedures where legal claims arise	20

3 Will trusts — 21

	3.1	Notification of interest	21
	3.2	Provision of estate administration accounts	21
	3.3	Valuation of trust assets and frequency of feedback	21
	3.4	Partition of a will trust – what charites are obliged to ask	22

4 Taxation — 23

4.1 Income tax — 23
- 4.1.1 Reclaiming income tax paid on estate income — 23
- 4.1.2 Form R185 (Estate income) — 23
- 4.1.3 Rate of tax reclaimable by the charity — 23
- 4.1.4 Administration expenses chargeable against income — 23
- 4.1.5 Deciding whether or not to produce Forms R185 (Estate income) — 24

4.2 Capital gains tax (CGT) — 24
- 4.2.1 Personal representatives' liability to CGT — 24
- 4.2.2 Personal representatives' Annual Exempt Amount — 24
- 4.2.3 Appropriating assets to charity beneficiaries — 25
- 4.2.4 Appropriating assets with or without the beneficiary's consent — 25
- 4.2.5 Appropriation of land to charity beneficiaries — 25

4.3 Inheritance Tax (IHT) — 26
- 4.3.1 *Ratcliffe* or *Benham* construction — 26
- 4.3.2 Grossing up — 27
- 4.3.3 How to show the IHT liability in the estate accounts — 27

4.4 Finance Bill 2012 reduction of IHT rate — 27
- 4.4.1 Reduced rate of IHT — 27
- 4.4.2 Components of an estate — 27
- 4.4.3 'Baseline amount' — 28
- 4.4.4 Merging of components — 28
- 4.4.5 Notifying the charity of a deed of variation — 28
- 4.4.6 Examples of the application of the lower 36 per cent IHT rate — 28

4.5 Bodies that do not benefit from tax concessions — 29

5 Other issues affecting charities and estates — 30

5.1 Charities as income beneficiaries — 30
5.2 Discretionary legacies — 30
5.3 Deeds of variation — 30
5.4 The transferable nil-rate band — 31

APPENDICES 33

A	**Example letter requesting a *Larke* v. *Nugus* statement**	33
B	**Will clauses**	35
	B1 Pecuniary bequest	35
	B2 Specific bequest	35
	B3 Residuary bequest	35
	B4 Wording to express a testator's wish	35
	B5 Wording to appoint a charity as executor	35
	B6 Wording for a bequest to a church	35
	B7 General cy-près clause	36
C	**Sample Smee & Ford notification**	37
D	**Royal Sign Manual directions**	38
E	**Memorandum of appropriation for investments**	42
F	**STEP draft model clause for wills benefitting a charity to satisfy the 10 per cent test**	43
G	**Further reading**	46
H	**Useful links**	47

About the contributors

The **Institute of Legacy Management** (ILM), familiar to many practitioners, provides a programme of accredited training and a forum for charity legacy professionals. ILM aims to encourage best practice in estate administration and provides an information service to approximately 500 individual members representing 300 charities and including solicitors in private practice. ILM does not have the power to sanction its members, but ILM's clear wish is that they should follow best practice.

The Law Society's Private Client Section (formerly the Probate Section) provides best practice information and support to those working in the fields of wills, financial planning, trusts, tax planning, Court of Protection, care planning and estate administration. The benefits of membership include a magazine, free seminars and webinars, e-alerts, website, networking opportunities and discounts on events and related products.

Contributors

Anthony Collinson, solicitor, Whiteside and Knowles, member of the Law Society's Private Client Section Executive Committee

Gary F. Rycroft, solicitor, Joseph A. Jones & Co., member of the Law Society's Private Client Section Executive Committee

Jane Whitfield, solicitor, Wellers Law Group LLP, member of the Law Society's Wills and Equity Committee

Jenny Franzmann F.Inst.L.Ex, RSPCA and Director of the Institute of Legacy Management

Roshana Gammampila LLB LLM, Director of the Institute of Legacy Management

Acknowledgements

The contributors would like to thank Paul Hewitt (Withers LLP) for his assistance with the drafting of various sections in this book.

Preface

This third edition of *Charities as Beneficiaries* has been updated by expert contributors drawn from the Private Client Section Executive Committee and Wills and Equity Committee of the Law Society, the Institute of Legacy Management, and solicitors in private practice.

In this book, the contributors explain the roles and obligations of solicitors and charity legacy managers in order to promote greater understanding of how these professionals can work together to maximise the efficiency and value of bequests to charity and minimise the cost of estate administration.

We would like to offer our thanks to the contributors who have given freely of their time to update this book and recommend their helpful and practical guidance to our members.

Patricia Wass
Chair, Law Society's Private Client Section

Brad Grieve
CEO, Institute of Legacy Management

Introduction

In the nine years since the first edition of this book was published, it is probably true to say that each reader has experienced at least one 'difficult probate'. The increase in the complexity and diversification of estates continues, with a knock-on effect on the work to be done and the problems encountered.

The aim of this book is to help both solicitors and charity legacy professionals to understand each other's needs and to use their expertise and resources to avoid or overcome these 'difficult probates'.

For solicitors, the diversity of assets, emergence of digital inheritance, variety and complexity of modern family structures and regulation of financial institutions provide an increasing number of hoops to jump through and bureaucracy to manage.

Following guidance from the Charity Commission and in recognition of the vital role that gifts left in wills play in the furtherance of their causes, charitable beneficiaries have in recent years taken a more professional attitude towards their legacy entitlements. They are conscious of their duty to optimise their benefit, while taking into account such discretion as they may have under the law.

Charity legacy professionals are able to offer solicitors ways in which monies can be maximised. In particular, they can offer suggestions on how best to utilise their charitable tax-exempt status and also put solicitors in touch with third parties, such as stockbrokers, auction houses and surveyors, who offer preferential rates when dealing with assets in estates which include charity beneficiaries.

The law is as stated on 15 May 2012.

Chapter 1

Drawing up wills

1.1 Introduction

Seventy-four per cent of people in the UK support charities during their lifetime and 7 per cent leave gifts to charities in their wills. These legacy gifts are valued at £2 billion per annum and they enable charitable work to be undertaken that would otherwise go unfunded. As will-drafters and executors, solicitors play a crucial part in ensuring this generosity achieves its purpose.

In addition to including specific charitable legacies in a will, a testator can also avoid the failure of gifts of residue (for example, if named beneficiaries cannot be traced) if the will contains a long-stop gift to charity or for charitable purposes.

1.2 Identifying a charity correctly

1.2.1 Verifying the name of the intended charity beneficiary

It is important that charities are correctly named. Many charities have similar names and, after the testator's death, the cost of verifying an intended but ambiguously named charity beneficiary can be significant. For this reason, the correct name of the charity as well as its registration number should always be stated. These will usually be quoted in literature that a client has received from a charity and can be checked using one of the following sources:

- The Charity Commission Register (**www.charity-commission.gov.uk**, tel. 0845 300 0218);
- Institute of Legacy Management (ILM) (**www.legacymanagement.org.uk**);
- Charity Choice (**www.charitychoice.co.uk**);
- The Law Society *Gazette*'s Charity & Appeals and Spring Legacy Appeals Directories and Charity Explorer online directory (**www.lawgazette.co.uk/charityexplorer**).

Certain organisations in England and Wales will not be listed on the Charity Commission Register. These include charities excepted by order or regulation, organisations that have an income which does not exceed £5,000 a year, and registered places of worship (see Charities Act 2011, Sched.3: Exempt charities).

1.2.2 Bequests to local branches or committees

In addition to ensuring that a charity's name and registration number are stated correctly, where a charity has local branches or committees, will-drafting solicitors should also consider the following:

- whether these branches or committees are recognised as separate entities capable of receiving legacy gifts in their own right;
- whether their client wishes to benefit the charity generally or a specific branch or committee.

Some charity branches and committees are unable under the constitution of their charity to receive legacy gifts (see also **1.7.2** below).

1.2.3 Specifying a particular project or purpose

The majority of legacy bequests to charity are left without specific instructions as to how they should be used. Such gifts are therefore applied to where the need is greatest within a charity's area of work. Development charities in particular have noted how such gifts have enabled them to respond to unforeseen disasters, such as the 2010 earthquake in Haiti.

A testator who has a good understanding of their chosen charity's work may specify a particular project or type of work towards which they wish their gift to be applied. For example, the testator may wish the money to be used in a particular unit at a hospital or towards a specific piece of research. In those circumstances, it is important that the solicitor contacts the charity concerned to ascertain the viability of this, as the project or type of work may have a planned end date. Other problems may arise if the specified object of the charity no longer exists when the testator dies, or the particular project is no longer in need of funds. The likelihood of such problems occurring is quite high, as it is common for a number of years to have passed between the drafting of the will and the receipt of the gift on death (see **1.2.4** below for the inclusion of a cy-près clause in wills).

Where support for a particular project or type of work is desired by the client, it is recommended that this is stated as a wish. This will enable the charity to apply the gift to an alternative project in the event that the specified work is no longer being carried out. It is advisable for the solicitor to speak with the relevant charity and request their recommended wording.

1.2.4 Cy-près

It is good practice to include a general cy-près clause providing the executors with the discretion to benefit a replacement charity in the event that:

(a) the purposes cannot be carried out according to the directions given and to the spirit of the gift;
(b) the original purposes provide a use for part only of the property available by virtue of the gift;
(c) the property available by virtue of the gift can be more effectively used in conjunction with other property applicable for similar purposes; or
(d) since the will was made, the original purposes have been adequately provided for by other means, or have ceased to be charitable at law, or have ceased in any other way to provide a suitable and effective method of using the property available by virtue of the gift.

See **Appendix B7** for an example clause.

> **Cy-près: An example**
>
> Mrs C bequeathed a share of her residuary estate to the 'Children's Holiday Fund' of a Christian missionary charity. However, at the date of Mrs C's death in 2011, the fund no longer existed. It had been established at a time when the majority of children of missionaries were sent to boarding school and was therefore used either to meet the costs of reuniting the children with their parents during the school holidays, or to enable the whole family to have a holiday together. By 2011 things had changed. Children of missionaries generally stay with their parents and either are home-educated or attend an English-speaking school in the local area.
>
> The executors applied to the Charity Commission for a scheme to allow the purposes for which the gift had been given to be extended to include providing support for missionary families, and in particular meeting the costs generally for missionaries of bringing up their children, including the children's allowances and education costs, but also providing for holidays where that would be appropriate. The charity also wanted to use some of the funds to pay for the travel costs of students studying in the UK whose parents were on the mission field, to enable the students to visit their parents during a university vacation.
>
> The Charity Commission decided, in reliance on *Re Finger's Will Trusts* [1971] 3 All ER 1050, that the gift to the Children's Holiday Fund was a gift for purposes and could therefore be saved by way of a scheme. The Commission was satisfied that it could be shown from the context of Mrs C's will:
>
> (a) that her intention to make the gift was not dependent upon the named fund being available at the time when the gift took effect to serve as the instrument for applying the subject-matter of the gift to the charitable purpose for which it was by inference given; and
> (b) that the particular charitable purpose still survives.

A will-drafter has three options to avoid the problem illustrated by the example:

- telephone the charity to check whether it is likely that the stated use will be able to be fulfilled (strongly recommended);
- express the gift as a wish rather than a direction (recommended); or
- include a cy-près clause (a good fail-safe).

1.2.5 Merged charities

When two or more charities have merged and the merger has been registered with the Charity Commission pursuant to the Charities Act 2011, s.305 then such a gift will automatically take effect as a gift to the successor body.

1.2.6 Is the organisation a charity?

A number of voluntary organisations are not charities. This might be because they wish to campaign or their primary purpose is political campaigning. Certain campaigning organisations may have formed charitable trusts to receive donations and legacies that would satisfy the charitable exempt status for tax purposes (see **Chapter 4**).

1.3 Charity will-making schemes

Schemes which exist to support testators in making gifts to charity include Will Aid and Remember a Charity.

1.3.1 Will Aid

Will Aid takes place annually in November. It aims to increase public awareness of the importance of charitable legacy giving. Under the scheme solicitors offer a will-writing service to members of the public but instead of paying the solicitor's fee, the client makes a donation which the solicitor sends to Will Aid. The donation is distributed among the nine participating charities. Participation in the scheme also provides firms with publicity and social responsibility opportunities. For further information visit **www.willaid.org.uk**.

1.3.2 Remember a Charity

Remember a Charity was formed in 2000. It is a consortium of over 140 UK charities that work together to encourage people to consider leaving a charitable gift in their will. For more information visit **www.rememberacharity.org.uk**.

1.3.3 Charities paying for wills

Some charities offer a scheme to pay the cost of preparing a will for an individual in expectation of receiving a legacy or in the course of carrying out its charitable purposes (e.g. in support of a terminally ill person). The Charity Commission states in *Paying for Wills with Charity Funds* ('the Guidance') that it has 'no objection in principle' to these schemes (see **www.charity-commission.gov.uk**).

In paras.18–20 of the Guidance, the Charity Commission recommends that charities take great care to avoid creating any contractual agreement with the solicitor's firm that prepares the will in order to avoid the risk that the charity might be regarded as having taken responsibility for the will. It advises charities to recommend the testator instructs their own solicitor or chooses a solicitor from a list available from the charity or from another source. Importantly, the charity should decline to recommend any particular firm or individual.

The Charity Commission stresses that the 'normal professional relationship must exist between the solicitor and the testator' (para.21). The testator is liable for the cost of preparation of the will but will be entitled to recover this cost from the charity, subject to the terms of the scheme set out in standard documentation. These terms may specify a pre-agreed maximum cost that will be met. The Charity Commission also recommends that no mention of a legacy to the charity is made in this documentation and it does not expect the will-drafting solicitor to suggest that the client benefits any charity.

The Guidance refers to the requirements of the Solicitors' Introduction and Referral Code 1990, which was revoked on 1 July 2007. A firm regulated by the SRA must act in accordance with the SRA Principles 2011 and the SRA Code of Conduct 2011 (O(1.6), IB(1.4), IB(1.5) and IB(1.16) are particularly relevant). The solicitor will also need to decide whether the individual circumstances of the instructions constitute a referral arrangement within the meaning given to these terms in the SRA Handbook Glossary 2011:

> **referral** includes any situation in which another person, business or organisation introduces or refers a client to your business, recommends your business to a client or otherwise puts you and a client in touch with each other.

arrangement in relation to ... referrals in Chapters 1, 6 and 9 of the SRA Code of Conduct, means any express or tacit agreement between you and another person, whether contractually binding or not.

If there is a referral arrangement, the outcomes and indicative behaviours in Chapter 9 of the SRA Code of Conduct 2011 will apply (see www.sra.org.uk for the most up-to-date version of the SRA Handbook). The following guidance, although not in force, may also be helpful:

- keep a written 'record' of any referral arrangement whether or not any financial arrangement is involved (Solicitors' Introduction and Referral Code 1990, s.2(9));
- 'agree with the introducer, when you enter into the agreement, the nature of the information to be given to the client, and ... keep a record of what you agree' (*Questions and Answers on Referral Fees*, Law Society, 2005)
- ensure that the information given to the client agreed by the solicitor and introducer includes express mention of the independence of the solicitor's professional advice (Solicitors' Introduction and Referral Code 1990, s.3(4)).

The Charity Commission's Guidance acknowledges that there are risks of legal challenge to wills when a charity offers to meet the cost of will preparation. It offers advice to charities at para.14 on the implementation of safeguards to minimise these risks:

> [W]e would normally expect charities to do what they reasonably can to ensure that:
>
> - written clarification is given to the testator and to the solicitor explaining the basis upon which the charity is offering to meet the cost of the preparation of the will and the procedures to be followed;
> - solicitors preparing a will make it plain to all concerned that they are acting exclusively in the interests of the testator, even though their cost will be met by the charity;
> - solicitors take instructions directly from the testator, rather than from the charity. Where possible, we recommend that these instructions are confirmed in writing;
> - before the will is executed the solicitor is satisfied that the testator fully understands the effect of the will and that it reflects his or her instructions, and that this is recorded.

At para.17, the Charity Commission also advises that:

> Charities may wish to seek written confirmation from any solicitor who prepares a will for a client at their expense that in any case where the testator after advice decides to leave a legacy to the charity, that they are fully satisfied that the testator:
>
> - was **not** subject to any influence;
> - **did** fully understand and intend what he or she was doing; and that
> - the charges made (indirectly) to the charity will correspond to those normally charged for preparing a will.

Provision of such information during the testator's lifetime will require consent from the testator.

1.4 Managing risk

1.4.1 Avoiding claims post-death

If a will excludes or makes limited provision for close family members, there is always a possibility of claims being issued or threatened post-death.

The need for a full attendance note when taking instructions for a will is particularly acute in such circumstances. Attendance notes should also be made of any contact with the testator during the will-making process, including (where the solicitor is involved) of the will being executed. There needs to be a clear record showing that the testator considered, for instance, the reasons for changing any preceding will, those who might expect/hope to benefit and, ideally, the reasons for benefiting the charities identified.

It may assist in some circumstances if the client discusses their wishes with family members (though for understandable reasons a client may well prefer to keep affairs private).

During their lifetime, a client may also wish to advise the benefiting charity of their intention to make a gift in their will. Certainly the charity is likely to find that contact, and similarly a record of lifetime support, will assist in upholding the client's wishes. In *Illott v. Mitson* [2011] EWCA Civ 346 the court placed importance on the fact that the testatrix did not appear to have had any connection with the animal welfare charities concerned during her lifetime, nor was there evidence that showed any particular love for animals.

1.4.2 *Larke* v. *Nugus* statements

Practitioners will be aware of their professional conduct obligations under which they can be required to produce a statement detailing the circumstances of the preparation of the will – known as a *Larke* v. *Nugus* statement. The Law Society's Practice Note: Disputed Wills (2011) gives guidance on this topic. An example of a letter requesting a *Larke* v. *Nugus* statement and setting out the requirements of the same is provided in **Appendix A**.

1.4.3 File retention and storage of the will

The Law Society's Practice Note: File Retention: Wills and Probate (2011) reminds solicitors that:

> When considering whether a file should be destroyed you should note that in will cases successful claims can be brought well after the usual contractual period of six years from the end of the retainer or time the work was completed/applicable in many other matters. Files should therefore be retained until any risk of a claim has passed. (para.6.1)

It is good practice for a solicitor who prepares a will to store the original until after the death of the client, or until the solicitor is able to return the original to the client. The solicitor's retainer should confirm what will happen to the original will and other supporting documentation that is not the firm's property. The solicitor should keep a copy of the will, even if the will is revoked or the solicitor believes or knows a later will has been made. The client also has the option, for a fee, to lodge a will with the Probate Registry for safe keeping.

1.4.4 Validity of wills in suspicious circumstances

Over recent years there have been high profile cases of will fraud where certain individuals took advantage of elderly clients and a will was changed shortly before a client's death. In some of these cases, it was to the detriment of charities who were former beneficiaries. As a result of this, charities are now more likely to question the making of a will when this occurs. In particular, they are likely to make a written request for further information regarding the circumstances behind the instructions for the will and also the execution of it.

Charities are increasingly aware of the risks of challenge or criticism where they provide assistance to vulnerable supporters. The Legacy Fundraising Code of Fundraising Practice (Institute of

Fundraising, 2007) gives guidance on related issues such as one-to-one fundraising (5.3), health, safety and risk management (5.4) and paying for wills with charity funds (7.4). Certain parts of the code are binding on charity members of the Institute and more than 90 per cent of large charities and the majority of medium-sized charities are members.

1.5 Charities and tax planning

1.5.1 Inheritance Tax (IHT)

The IHT concession to charities has long been enshrined in law because of the work charities undertake for the benefit of society. All legacies to charities usually attract full IHT exemption (see **Chapter 4**). The inclusion of charitable gifts in a will can therefore substantially reduce the IHT burden on an estate.

1.5.2 Foreign charities

A legacy to a foreign charity established outside the UK will not benefit from IHT concessions (see **Chapter 4**) unless the charity:

- is established elsewhere in the European Union, in Norway or in Iceland (or any other jurisdiction subsequently approved by regulations); and
- meets the other tests for a UK charity to be accepted as a charity for tax purposes.

To be accepted as a charity for tax purposes, the charity must be:

- established for charitable purposes only (as determined under English law);
- registered with any regulator with which its own law requires it to be registered; and
- managed by 'fit and proper' persons.

There are also two further alternatives open to the client:

- a gift may be made to a UK charity carrying out the charitable work envisaged overseas, or which funds a local organisation doing so; or
- a bequest may be made to a donor-advised fund (such as the Charities Aid Foundation) with a letter of wishes stating how the client wishes the money to be spent. It is important to appreciate, however:
  - the funds cannot be transferred overseas unless proper steps have been taken by the donor-advised fund to ensure that any recipient organisation will use them only for purposes which are charitable under English law; and
  - the decision to make such an onwards transfer will lie with the donor-advised fund.

1.6 Charities as executors

Some charities may agree to act as executor where a gift has been left to them in a will, and in doing so they can reduce the costs of an estate administration. However, because the role of an executor is onerous, in practice charities are only able to justify the application of resources if they receive a substantial benefit under the will.

The way in which charities are able to carry out the role of executor varies depending on whether they have trust corporation status. A charity with such status can be nominated as executor and can carry out the duties of this role in its corporate capacity. A charity without trust corporation status may specify a particular post-holder to take on this role in an individual capacity and as the occupant of a particular post within the charity.

In terms of the wording to be used in the will to appoint a charity as executor:

- Where the charity has trust corporation status, the charity's full name and registration number will suffice. (A trust corporation may also suggest its own form of wording for the appointment, including provisions for remuneration.)
- For a charity without trust corporation status it is sensible to first contact the charity and ask for the designation of the post charged with performing executory duties on behalf of that charity. The naming of an individual employee as executor should be avoided as that person may no longer be working for the charity at the time of the testator's death.

See **Appendix B5** for suggested wording to appoint a charity as executor.

Unless a charity has trust corporation status it may not receive remuneration for acting as executor, although it may be reimbursed for reasonable out-of-pocket expenses. A charity with trust corporation status may charge for its time, but in practice few charities do so, in expectation of receiving the legacy.

Often charity legacy teams may not have the capacity to carry out all the duties involved in an executorship or may be concerned about the potential liability in doing so, and therefore many instruct solicitors to carry out at least some estate administration activities on their behalf. Even where this is the case, the cost of the estate administration may be reduced if charities carry out the time-consuming elements, thereby limiting the legal fees incurred.

1.7 Application of funds left to charity

1.7.1 Trusts for those with special needs

Several charities, such as Mencap and Mind, can provide specific information on the most appropriate types of trusts for people with special needs. These trusts not only take the best advantage of trust income, but also ensure that vulnerable beneficiaries are protected as far as possible.

1.7.2 Bequests to branches of national charities

The status of a charity's branches (or local committees) depends on the constitution of the particular organisation. While some charities' branches are registered as entities in their own right, others may be representatives of the main organisation with a mandate limited to fundraising. In the latter case, branches (or local committees) will not have the power to apply funds themselves. For this reason and because, under the Accounting and Reporting by Charities: Statement of Recommended Practice (Charity Commission, 2005), charities are obliged to clearly separate restricted income (e.g. income for use by a particular branch) from unrestricted income in their published accounts, it is important that solicitors clearly capture their client's intentions.

The following should be clarified when drafting a clause involving a branch of a charity:

- Does the client mean for the funds to pass through the branch or local committee on their way to being spent according to the needs of the charity as a whole?
- Does the client wish the funds to be used locally with the proviso that, if they are not used locally, the legacy would fail? If this is the case, clients should also be asked to clarify what should happen if, at the date of death, the local branch no longer exists.
- Does the client mean to permit the charity to apply the funds elsewhere if the branch or committee no longer exists at the date of death?
- What is the status of the branch (is it a separate registered charity or simply a local fundraising operation)? If it is not a separate charity then the legacy will have to be paid to the trustees of the national charity, although the trustees may be under an obligation to apply the gift to any particular purposes specified by the testator.

In order to ensure that the gift can be received and applied as intended by the client, it is important for solicitors to contact the charities concerned to ascertain how best to give effect to their client's wishes.

It is also important to note the differences in the following wordings for a clause involving a branch of a charity as these give effect to very different bequests:

- 'I LEAVE the sum of £N to XYZ Charity, Penrith Branch.'
- 'I LEAVE for the use of XYZ Charity, Penrith Branch, the sum of £N.'
- 'I LEAVE XYZ Charity the sum of £N to be paid to its Penrith Branch.'
- 'I LEAVE XYZ Charity the sum of £N with the wish that it be for the benefit of the Penrith Branch.'

For the same reasons outlined in **1.2.3** it is also advisable for the testator's intention to be expressed as a wish rather than a direction.

1.8 Alternative ways to benefit charities

Clients who wish to benefit charitable causes but are unsure as to which specific charities they would like to nominate as beneficiaries may choose to make a gift to the Charities Aid Foundation (CAF). CAF distributes funds to a number of UK charities (see www.cafonline.org for details). If a letter of wishes specifying a particular charitable cause is included, CAF will ensure that only charities working to further that cause benefit from the client's legacy.

1.9 Executors' costs and expenses

The issue of remuneration for executors and the reimbursement of their expenses can create friction where a lay executor assumes that they are entitled to claim payment for time spent.

In accordance with the Trustee Act 2000, ss.28 and 29, a solicitor who is appointed to act as executor of an estate can charge fees, even if the will is silent on this point. A lay executor on the other hand is not allowed to charge fees or receive any remuneration for acting as executor (see **2.6.2** below).

All executors are entitled, however, to be reimbursed for reasonable expenses incurred whilst carrying out their duties. To manage expectations, therefore, solicitors are advised to explain to clients that lay executors are only entitled to claim for reasonable out-of-pocket expenses (see **2.6.3** below).

In recognition that a lay executor cannot receive any remuneration, it is possible for the testator to include a legacy to a lay executor which is conditional upon that executor proving the will.

1.10 Statutory will applications

An application may be made to the Court of Protection for an order to authorise the execution of a 'statutory will' for a person who lacks testamentary capacity. The power of the court to authorise the execution of a will for a person who lacks capacity derives from the Mental Capacity Act 2005, s.18(1)(i).

If a statutory will application is proposed whereby an existing charitable benefit is to be removed or reduced, the charity concerned should be notified at an early stage. The charity has an obligation to examine why the benefactor's existing testamentary wishes should be overridden.

In certain cases a deputy or an attorney may consider that it is in the best interests of the individual who lacks capacity to benefit a charity. This may be the case, for instance, where the deputy or attorney is aware that the individual has or had a connection with the charity (or the charity now provides some support). See further: *Re P* [2009] EWHC 163 (Ch); *ITW* v. *Z and M* [2009] EWHC 2525 (Fam) and *VAC* v. *JAD and others* [2010] EWHC 2159 (COP).

Chapter 2

Administration of estates

2.1 Notification of benefit

2.1.1 Communicating with charity beneficiaries

It is recommended that charity beneficiaries are notified of an interest in a will or codicil as early as possible. This is appreciated by charities for a number of reasons:

- Often a charity's trustees will have delegated authority to issue valid receipt of a bequest to a specific individual or legacy management team. Where a charity has a number of contact points (shops, regional offices, local supporter branches, etc.), early notification enables the nominated charity legacy professional to correspond with the executor and ensure that payment is received by the correct part of the charity.
- Legacy gifts account for a substantial part of many charities' income and early notification will help a charity to plan.
- Those who leave bequests to charities may have also been supporters of those charities during their lifetime. They may therefore have subscribed to charity newsletters and may receive mailings about fundraising appeals. When executors inform a charity of a legacy gift, the charity takes steps to ensure that no further correspondence is sent to the deceased supporter's address. Receiving charity mailings once a loved one has passed away can cause distress and charities rely on executors to help them avoid this situation.

It is considered good practice to provide residuary beneficiaries with a copy will at an early stage, usually on the understanding that it remains confidential until probate is granted.

2.1.2 Smee & Ford notification

Previously, the charity division of the Principal Probate Registry notified all charities when they were named in a will. Now this service is performed by a commercial organisation, Smee & Ford Ltd. All large and many medium-sized charities subscribe to this service, which covers probates in England and Wales and confirmations in Scotland. Following the grant (or confirmation), Smee & Ford supplies the subscribing charity with a synopsis of the grant, plus a summary of the benefit mentioned in the will. It does not supply a copy of the will or codicil(s), nor financial information other than the gross and net estate values sworn for probate. An example of a Smee & Ford notification is shown in **Appendix C**.

2.2 Terms and conditions letters

A solicitor's client must be given written notification of likely charges and fees in accordance with the provisions of the SRA Handbook. When the executors of a will, and thus the legal clients, are the partners/directors of a solicitors' firm or other entity regulated by the SRA, solicitors are encouraged to provide the usual fee information to residuary beneficiaries (see also **2.6.2**).

The Law Society's Practice Note: Appointment of a Professional Executor (2011) anticipates that where a solicitor has been appointed executor the client was provided with an indication of the likely costs and whether the costs will be calculated on the basis of an hourly rate or a percentage of the estate.

2.3 The Royal Sign Manual procedure

The Royal Sign Manual is literally the signature of the monarch (although now delegated to the Attorney General). The Royal Sign Manual procedure is used to identify charitable beneficiaries whose identity is uncertain. It is used when a legacy is made for charitable purposes but no particular objects or trustees have been named by the testator, for example, 'cancer research', 'heart research', etc. It can also be used when it appears that an organisation has been named, but on further investigation no charity exists with that name, for example, 'The Heart and Chest Foundation'.

The procedure cannot be used when it is possible to construe the will to identify the charity, nor can it be used to resolve a dispute over the validity or construction of the will.

If a trust has been interposed on the legacy, the correct procedure is to apply to the Charity Commission for a scheme, since the Royal Sign Manual procedure only applies in the case of a direct gift.

A Royal Sign Manual direction does not prevent third parties from claiming they are beneficially entitled to the gift but in the absence of any claim being notified executors can act in reliance on the direction.

It is for the executors to apply to the Attorney General for a Royal Sign Manual direction. In the first instance they should write to the Treasury Solicitor (see **Appendix D** for the address) with an original copy grant and will, any other evidence as to the charity the testator intended (e.g. records of donations made to a charity, evidence of a legacy pledge made to a charity, or evidence from friends or relatives), together with details of the value of the gift. The Attorney General, acting under authority delegated by the Queen, may direct that the bequest be made to a specific charity which most closely represents the testator's intention.

See **Appendix D** for further information on this procedure.

2.4 Rights of charity beneficiaries to information

Beneficiaries' rights are limited, in theory, to having the estate properly administered. Beneficiaries may take steps to enforce these rights, for example, by bringing an action for account under the Administration of Estates Act 1925, s.25. In addition, beneficiaries also have rights as far as the citation or removal of executors is concerned.

Charity legacy professionals have obligations to their trustees and the beneficiaries of their work, which a private individual does not have. They must comply with charity law or face the censure of the Charity Commission. In order to so comply, they require information that shows their charities are seeking their proper entitlement from an estate.

It is generally considered good practice for executors to provide residuary beneficiaries (whether charitable or not) with sufficient information to enable them to be satisfied that their proper entitlement has been received.

Regardless of the type of legacy, a charity will require the following information:

- name of the testator;
- the testator's last address;
- the date of death;
- the nature of the bequest.

What is required in addition to this information will depend on the type of bequest (see below).

2.4.1 Pecuniary legacies

Pecuniary legacies are the most straightforward types of gift and they attract the fewest number of requests for information from charities. In addition to the standard information set out above, an executor need only provide a charity with a copy of the will clause containing the bequest.

Where a pecuniary legacy is not received within the 'executor's year', which runs from the first anniversary of death, beneficiaries are entitled to receive statutory interest payable at the basic rate of funds in court. Such interest will accrue from the first day after the anniversary of death. Charity legacy professionals are aware of this entitlement and may request it.

2.4.2 Specific legacies

The type and nature of specific gifts can vary widely and therefore so too does the information that will be required by a charity beneficiary. Regardless of the nature of the specific legacy, an executor should provide a charity with a copy of the will clause containing the bequest.

Where the bequest is of commercial value, a charity will require the information needed to ascertain the financial value of the gift. The most common examples of gifts of value and the usual requirements are set out at **2.4.3** below.

Depending on their individual policies, charities may wish to take specific gifts *in specie* (see **2.5.3** below). Where they require executors sell such gifts on their behalf, charities are often able to provide details of valuers and agents who offer preferential commission rates. Where a specifically bequeathed asset is split between a number of beneficiaries, not all of which are charities, these preferential rates may benefit them all. It is recommended that practitioners consult charity legacy professionals.

2.4.3 Residuary legacies

Nearly 90 per cent of the £2 billion bequeathed to charity in the UK each year comes from residuary gifts. Because residuary values are variable, charities will require more detailed information when receiving such gifts. The information that charities will require is set out in (a)–(e) below.

(a) **A photocopy of the will and any codicils**

This is required so that the entitlement of the charity is clear to its trustees and auditors. It is good practice to supply these as a matter of course when first advising the charity beneficiary of its entitlement. When probate is granted, the charity will also appreciate a photocopy of the grant.

(b) **A schedule of assets and liabilities**

Understanding the composition of the estate in which it has a residuary share enables a charity to:

(i) assess the likely value of the legacy which will be paid to it and consider how the funds might be best applied (this is an essential part of a charity's financial planning);

(ii) identify any assets that may attract tax concessions and alert executors to this;

(iii) assist the executors in the disposal of certain assets. As mentioned in **2.4.2**, charities are often able to provide details of valuers and agents who offer them preferential commission rates.

It may save on extra work and expense if the charities simply receive a copy of HM Revenue and Customs Form IHT205 (Return of estate information) or Form IHT400 (Inheritance Tax account). Form IHT205 is used where the gross value of the estate is under £1 million and there is no IHT to pay because of spouse, civil partner or charity exemption. If Form IHT205 has been used it is useful to provide a breakdown of the summary figures.

(c) **Valuations of significant assets**

For the same reason that charity beneficiaries require a schedule of assets and liabilities, where there are valuable assets in an estate, charity legacy professionals are likely to request information about the financial value. The usual requirements are set out in the table below.

Asset	Usual requirement
Stocks and shares	A copy of a recent portfolio valuation
Shares in a private company	A copy of the latest audited accounts
Antiques and paintings	A copy of a valuation by a specialist valuers
Property	Copies of the estate agent's marketing valuations (preferably two for comparison) and, where requested, a valuation and report by registered chartered surveyor

As the executors and the beneficiaries have an interest in maximising the value of an estate it is advisable that executors proactively provide charities with the information they request.

Some charities will wish to have their share of any holdings transferred to their own portfolios, although this may not be appropriate if the shares conflict with their purpose. For example, medical research charities may choose not to take on tobacco company shares, and animal charities may similarly not take shares in companies which undertake vivisection. It is helpful to such charities if the estate administrators contact them first to elicit their views. Information regarding unusual or valuable assets may also be requested by charities.

(d) **A copy of the estate accounts**
See **2.6** below.

(e) **Form R185 (Estate income): statement of income from estates**

At the end of an estate administration, executors or their representatives should provide charitable residuary beneficiaries with HM Revenue and Customs Form R185 (Estate income). This enables the charities, as income tax exempt beneficiaries, to reclaim at least part of the income tax paid during the estate administration period.

This income is important to charities and, when aggregated, it can be substantial. For example, each year Save the Children UK is able to reclaim £50,000 in this way. For this reason, charity legacy professionals will often not consider an estate administration complete until they have received Form R185 (Estate income).

2.5 Common themes where charities are residuary beneficiaries

2.5.1 Consulting charities before agreeing the sale of estate assets

While there is no obligation on executors to seek the approval of residuary beneficiaries when disposing of assets, it is advisable for executors and their representatives to inform charity residuary beneficiaries of their intended course of action. Charity legacy professionals will often be able to help executors to ensure that the maximum value is achieved on the sale of assets and, in this way, help to ensure that the duty of the executors and their representatives is carried out.

2.5.2 Liaising with a number of charities

When there are numerous residuary beneficiary charities and there is a particular question on which the charities are required to reach a consensus, the charities may choose from amongst themselves a 'lead charity' to collate the charities' views and relay this information to the executors or solicitors on behalf of the group. The lead charity is not able to speak in place of the other charities, its role is merely to collate and convey information, thereby saving the time and effort of the executors and their representatives.

If there is no particular issue that requires discussion between the charities, the executors and their representatives should communicate updates and other necessary information directly to all the charities. Communicating such updates by round robin email could help minimise the costs of the estate administration.

2.5.3 Transferring assets *in specie*

Depending on their internal policies and portfolios, some charities may wish to have their portion of any shareholdings transferred to them directly rather than receiving the sale proceeds.

2.5.4 Chattels requested by family or friends

If the residue of an estate is left to one or more charities and a family member asks if they can have a particular item not otherwise mentioned in the will, most charities will agree, provided that the item is not of significant value. A guideline operated by some charities is that if no single item is thought to be worth more than £150, then it may pass to a family member. This is a guideline only; executors and their representatives must contact the residuary beneficiaries to seek their consent. Where it is possible that the requested item could be valuable, charity legacy professionals will often first request a valuation.

2.6 Estate accounts

2.6.1 Legacy professionals' queries

Given the right to obtain an action to account under the Administration of Estates Act 1925, s.25, it is considered standard practice for residuary beneficiaries to be provided with a copy of the estate accounts.

Charity legacy professionals are obliged by the Charity Commission to ensure that their organisations receive the full value of their entitlements for the benefit of their charitable objects. They are therefore diligent in reviewing estate accounts and will raise queries where there is a lack of clarity. Charity legacy professionals appreciate that this can cause additional work for executors and their representatives and are grateful for any clarification provided.

The types of issues a charity legacy professional might query after reviewing the estate accounts include:

- whether a calculation is correct;
- whether the terms of the will have been correctly applied;
- whether the estate, for IHT purposes, is affected by any lifetime gifts;
- any discrepancies in the values or composition of the estate assets between the final estate accounts and the schedule of assets and liabilities or forms IHT200/IHT205;
- whether charity tax concessions have been correctly applied;
- any deductions not authorised by the will or by agreement;
- the level of fees;
- whether money on deposit (in the client account) has been earning interest;
- whether the calculation and apportionment of IHT is correct (in particular, where there are both exempt and non-exempt residuary beneficiaries);
- the nature and extent of estate administration costs and expenses.

2.6.2 Fees

Where solicitors are the sole executors and they are administering the estate, they are the firm's own client. However, it makes good commercial sense and will assist in reducing the risk of complaints if the residuary beneficiaries are treated as if they are clients. It is therefore recommended that a solicitor, at the commencement of the estate administration, provides the residuary beneficiaries with the timetable and fee information usually included in a client care letter. Doing so ensures that all parties have shared expectations, and this should enable misunderstandings to be avoided as the administration progresses. Interim invoices can also be rendered. Where the client is a lay executor, a prudent solicitor, with the agreement of their client, would also provide this information to all residuary beneficiaries.

Article 3 of the Solicitors' (Non-Contentious Business) Remuneration Order 2009, SI 2009/1931 states that in non-contentious business '[a] solicitor's costs must fair and reasonable having regard to all the circumstances of the case'. Solicitors are also referred to *Non-Contentious Costs* (Law Society, 2011) and the Court of Appeal decision and guidance in *Jemma Trust v. Liptrott* [2003] EWCA Civ 1476. Solicitors will also be aware that an application may be made to the court for an assessment of a solicitor's costs under the Solicitors Act 1974, ss.70 and 71.

In practice, most charity beneficiaries will accept fees that are supported by a detailed invoice which demonstrates that the chargeable time has been reasonably spent. As with most areas in charity legacy administration, it is lack of information rather than any fundamental objection that is likely to trigger queries.

2.6.3 Executors' expenses

It is settled law that trustees must not profit from their office and that they act purely voluntarily (*Re Barber* (1886) 34 Ch D 77). Thus, while lawyers are allowed to charge for estate administrations, lay executors are not.

Executors are allowed to be reimbursed for reasonable out-of-pocket expenses. These include, for example, the cost of obtaining death certificates and reasonable travel expenses. Executors' out-of-pocket expenses should be itemised in the accounts and the relevant receipts should be kept in the estate administration file. Lay executors advised of this at an early stage may choose to renounce their role or simply take a less active role in the administration if they so wish.

It is important to note that while lay executors may not charge for their own time, they may employ and remunerate another layperson to carry out the tasks of an estate administration.

2.6.4 IHT and its apportionment

Given their tax-exempt status, charities look carefully at the way in which IHT has been treated as an expense in estate accounts.

The first issue to be addressed is the amount of tax that has been paid. As such, the accounts should indicate whether additional tax has been paid due to there having been lifetime gifts or aggregable funds or, alternatively, whether reliefs such as agricultural property relief or business property relief have been claimed.

The accounts should also clearly set out the apportionment of the tax. In particular, solicitors should be aware that, following the decision in *Re Ratcliffe (deceased)* (1999) STC 262, charity legacy professionals will always check that the provisions of the Inheritance Tax Act 1984, s.41(b) have been applied. For further details, see **4.3**.

The accounts should accurately show that the correct beneficiaries have paid the correct tax and that the charities' share has been calculated as being tax exempt (see **Chapter 4**). Charity legacy professionals will often be able to provide guidance as to the calculation and apportionment of tax. Further information is available online at:

- ILM (www.legacymanagement.org.uk); and
- HM Revenue and Customs (www.hmrc.gov.uk), including a tax calculator.

2.6.5 Indemnities

Executors are entitled to be reasonably confident that they will not face personal liability after an estate administration is concluded. An executor who has placed advertisements for claimants (pursuant to the Trustee Act 1925, s.27) and subsequently distributes the estate in accordance with the will may not be held personally liable for a claim against the estate subsequently communicated. The claimant's remedy lies against the beneficiaries. Thus, open-ended indemnities are simply not needed. Charities are also unlikely to agree where executors seek wide indemnities when the only real cause for concern is a specific contingency, or where the executors say they are concerned about the possibility of a liability arising of which they do not even have notice.

A charity may agree to give an indemnity in order to save the costs of a court application. For instance, rather than see the estate incur the cost of an application dealing with a legacy to a missing beneficiary, or where there is a possible personal injury claim (but the putative claimant has given no indication of pursuing such a claim), it is more likely to be cost effective to indemnify the executors.

A charity will wish any indemnity to be limited to the value which the charity has actually received (and pro rata to the charity's share of residue). It will also wish to avoid 'joint and several' liability because otherwise it will be assuming liability on behalf of others who are not objects of the charity.

Charities will wish to minimise the apparent volume of contingent liabilities. Therefore, a time limit could be included so that there is a defined point at which the indemnity may be deleted from the charity's register. For instance, if the indemnity is in relation to a potential breach of contract by the testator, there is no reason for the executors to expect an indemnity to last beyond six years from the date of the alleged breach.

2.7 Claims against estates in which charities share residue

2.7.1 Ex gratia claims

The funds of a charity must be applied to its charitable purpose. Therefore, when funds are left to charity, charity trustees are obliged to ensure that the entirety of funds are applied towards the charity's objects, meaning that a charity cannot agree to anything that is not a valid testamentary expense or bequest under the will. Any other payment can amount to an ex gratia payment if there is no legal basis for it to be made.

It was previously considered that charities could not agree this type of payment. However in *Re Snowden* [1970] Ch 700, it was decided that charities may make ex gratia payments, but only on the sanction of the court or the Attorney General. The judge ruled that the power to authorise an ex gratia payment was:

not to be exercised lightly or on slender grounds, but only in cases where it can be fairly said that if the charity were an individual it would be morally wrong of him to refuse to make the payment.

An application for authorisation to make an ex gratia payment is made to the Charity Commission, which has the power to authorise payments under the supervision of the Attorney General (Charities Act 2011, s.106).

The term 'ex gratia payment' has no precise legal meaning but is used in this sense to apply to a payment that the charity trustees:

- are under no legal obligation to make; but
- feel morally obliged to make; and
- cannot justify being in the interests of the charity; and
- have no power under the governing document of the charity to make.

Typical examples of such payments are:

- requests for the implementation of testamentary wishes that have not been properly executed;
- cases in which, by some operation of the law, a charity benefits significantly more than the testator intended to the detriment of a private individual.

If there is a legal claim, an ex gratia payment cannot be made unless it would be wholly disproportionate for a legal claim to be brought. Instead, the matter should be handled by way of compromise (see **2.7.2.** below on legal claims).

It may be argued that Charities Act 2011, s.105 is available to permit charities to use discretion where they are able to justify a payment as being 'expedient in the interests of the charity'. However, the Charity Commission examines each application carefully, as all such applications must have its approval.

Generally, a charity's legacy management team will act as a first screening point for all requests for ex gratia payments. Often, such teams have guidelines laid down by their trustees as to the type of claim on which they are likely to agree. They will also be well aware of the claims likely to be approved by the Charity Commission.

Charity legacy professionals generally have authority from their trustees to assess ex gratia requests and will also normally contact the other residuary beneficiary charities involved to assess their views.

If it is felt that a request has merit, the charity's trustees will need to receive certain information. They may take independent legal advice and, if they feel morally obliged to make the payment, they will apply to the Charity Commission for authorisation. The Charity Commission does not grant these applications lightly. It will require detailed evidence of the testator's intentions and why the will does not give effect to those intentions.

See further: *CC7 – Ex Gratia Payments by Charities* (Charity Commission, 2001) and *OG11 – Operational Guidance: Ex Gratia Payments by Charities* (Charity Commission) available at **www.charitycommission.gov.uk**.

2.7.2 Charity procedures where legal claims arise

Where a claim is brought against an estate in which there are beneficiary charities, they should be informed as soon as possible and provided with full information on the nature of the claim and the potential impact on their entitlement. In the spirit of the Civil Procedure Rules and *ACTAPS Practice Guidance Notes for the Resolution of Trust and Probate Disputes* (Association of Contentious Trust and Probate Specialists, 2006), better known as the ACTAPS Code, it will be advantageous to all parties if a settlement can be negotiated before proceedings are issued.

Charities are conscious of their duty to receive their full entitlement and, understandably, they are also conscious of the importance of avoiding conflict. So that they can be confident that they strike a good balance between these concerns, charities will usually seek independent legal advice.

Indeed, it would normally be appropriate for the charity beneficiaries to take over the conduct of the claim or subsequent litigation, allowing the executors to maintain a position of neutrality.

Chapter 3

Will trusts

3.1 Notification of interest

As mentioned in **2.1.2** above, Smee & Ford Ltd advises subscribing charities when they are named in a will. It will also advise subscribing charities when they are named as remaindermen in a will trust.

3.2 Provision of estate administration accounts

Although the benefit of a reversionary interest does not materialise until the falling-in of the will trust, the value of that interest depends on both the initial value of the trust fund and its management during the life of the trust. A charity that does not have a record of how the initial fund was created could be criticised by the Charity Commission for failing to protect its entitlement. For this reason, charity legacy professionals will often ask for a copy of the estate administration accounts, which are regarded as a trust document.

3.3 Valuation of trust assets and frequency of feedback

During the life of the will trust, remaindermen charities may ask for updates on the value of the trust assets. This is particularly likely where the fund is comprised of investments. It is good practice for trustees to provide remainder beneficiaries with an up-to-date trust portfolio valuation once a year. Where trust assets are in the form of property, charities will require confirmation that it remains insured and maintained.

In choosing investments, trustees should hold a balance as between beneficiaries interested in income and those interested in capital, unless there is express contrary wording in the settlement. Prudent trustees will advise remaindermen when there is a material change in the composition of the trust assets or a change in the trustees. If, for instance, the will trust includes a property, and the will allows the trustees to replace it with one that may be more suitable for the life tenant, the remaindermen should be advised of the changes proposed and provided with valuations of the respective properties.

When a will trust falls-in by virtue of the death of the life tenant, there may be a delay in distribution of benefit because of the need to deal with the life tenant's own estate.

Where the trust property has to be sold following the falling-in of the trust because it vests automatically in a remainderman charity, the Charities Act 2011, ss.117–123 are invoked. See **Chapter 4**.

3.4 Partition of a will trust – what charities are obliged to ask

Sometimes the life tenant or the remainderman of a trust wishes to partition the trust and bring it to an end. The life tenant may be in need of a capital sum and/or there may be IHT savings to be made by such a partition. Charities are generally willing to look at the possibility and often welcome the acceleration of their interest.

In order to partition the trust correctly and fairly, an actuarial valuation should be obtained and the recommendations therein should be supported by a medical report confirming that the life tenant's health is as assumed for the purposes of the valuation. In the interest of ensuring that their charities comply with their duty to receive the entirety of their entitlements, charity legacy professionals will request that these steps are taken. The cost of this should normally be borne by the trust fund, or otherwise by the charities and life tenant by agreement.

It is possible for partitions of very small funds to be undertaken without an actuarial valuation where the cost of valuation would be disproportionate to the value of the fund.

Chapter 4

Taxation

4.1 Income tax

4.1.1 Reclaiming income tax paid on estate income

Charities can reclaim income tax paid on most of the income received during the administration period. This includes gross income (such as rent from property, or money received into a client account) on which the tax is then paid by the executors to HM Revenue and Customs. One of the exceptions is dividend payments from shareholdings. Charities cannot claim a repayment of the tax credit attaching to any dividends they receive, although the dividend payments should still be included on the income certificate provided to the charity by the executors (see below).

4.1.2 Form R185 (Estate income)

The personal representatives should provide a signed certificate of income to each charity beneficiary, using the prescribed Form R185 (Estate income). A certificate must be provided for each year in which there is a distribution; a distribution for these purposes will include an appropriation. If no distribution is made, the income (and the tax deemed to have been paid by the beneficiaries) is rolled up until such time as a distribution is made.

When distributions are made to beneficiaries from an estate, the beneficiaries are deemed to have been paid income first, followed by capital. The Income Tax (Trading and Other Income) Act 2005 contains the rules governing estate income.

4.1.3 Rate of tax reclaimable by the charity

The rate of tax reclaimable by the charity is not the tax actually borne by the income, but the rate in force for the year in which the income is distributed. Accordingly, it can be helpful to make annual distributions together with the appropriate Form R185 (Estate income) certificates. Many charity legacy professionals will be experienced in completing Form R185 (Estate income) certificates and may be able to offer assistance in more complex estates. Useful information is also given on HM Revenue and Customs website (**www.hmrc.gov.uk**).

It is advisable for personal representatives to structure the estate accounts so that estate income (both gross and net) is shown in a separate income account, broken down according to tax year.

4.1.4 Administration expenses chargeable against income

As mentioned above, income received by the personal representatives suffers basic rate tax or savings rate tax either by deduction at source or by direct assessment in their hands. Personal representatives are permitted to reduce the measure of income certified to beneficiaries in the Form

R185 (Estate income) by deducting a percentage of the income to represent administration expenses. Informally, it is accepted that a deduction of 10 per cent is usually allowed by HM Revenue and Customs, but each estate will be different and this should not be taken as a fixed percentage.

If the personal representatives have discretion to deduct administration expenses from income or capital, the personal representatives should consider the charity beneficiary's tax position. As charities are able to reclaim most of the income tax paid by the personal representatives, it may be advisable for the personal representatives to deduct expenses from capital so as not to prejudice any claim the charity beneficiary may have for a repayment of income tax.

4.1.5 Deciding whether or not to produce Forms R185 (Estate income)

It is important for personal representatives to weigh up the benefit of producing Forms R185 (Estate income). In estates of modest value where the amount of tax that can be reclaimed by the charity is minimal, the cost of producing Forms R185 (Estate income) may outweigh the benefit to the charity. On the other hand, tax reclaimed by charities can add a considerable amount to the charity's funds.

4.2 Capital gains tax (CGT)

4.2.1 Personal representatives' liability to CGT

Personal representatives are liable to CGT if capital assets are sold from the estate. When personal representatives take control of the deceased's assets, the assets are treated as if the personal representatives had acquired them at their market value at the date of death.

When an asset is transferred to a beneficiary under the will or under the rules of intestacy, personal representatives are not treated as disposing of it for CGT purposes. Instead, the beneficiary is treated as having acquired the asset on the date of death at its value for IHT if there was liability, or otherwise at its market value on that date.

Sometimes it may be necessary to sell assets during the administration period, for example, to raise money to pay IHT or to settle cash legacies. If so, the personal representatives will have to declare any chargeable gains made, and pay CGT out of estate funds. CGT is chargeable only on gains arising between the date of death and when the assets are sold.

4.2.2 Personal representatives' Annual Exempt Amount

Personal representatives are entitled to the Annual Exempt Amount for the tax year in which the death occurred and the following two tax years. After that, there is no tax-free allowance against gains during the administration period.

The Annual Exempt Amount for personal representatives is £10,600 for the 2011/12 tax year and will remain at this amount for the 2012/13 tax year. After that, the Annual Exempt Amount is due to rise in line with the consumer price index instead of the retail price index, unless the government overrides this.

For gains made on or before 22 June 2010, CGT is charged to personal representatives at a flat rate of 18 per cent. For gains made after 22 June 2010, CGT is charged at 28 per cent.

4.2.3 Appropriating assets to charity beneficiaries

CGT can be mitigated by appropriating an asset to a beneficiary or beneficiaries prior to sale. The personal representatives then sell as bare trustees, with the beneficiaries accounting direct to HM Revenue and Customs for any CGT due on their share of that asset. In the case of a charity beneficiary, the charity is exempt from tax on capital gains providing the proceeds of the disposal are used for charitable purposes.

Personal representatives may appropriate an asset to one or more beneficiaries as soon as it is known that the asset is not required to pay the debts of the estate and costs during the administration period.

The Administration of Estates Act 1925, s.41 allows personal representatives to appropriate an asset either in full or in part satisfaction of a legacy or entitlement, provided the beneficiary consents to such appropriation. That said, many wills exclude the requirement contained in s.41 for the personal representatives to obtain the beneficiaries' consent, although it should be noted that s.41(5) provides that personal representatives should take into account the needs of all of the beneficiaries when exercising the power of appropriation.

4.2.4 Appropriating assets with or without the beneficiary's consent

Unless the will specifically authorises otherwise, the value of the asset for distribution purposes will be the value at the date of appropriation and not the value at the date of death. In addition, the power of appropriation is not available if the value of the asset exceeds the value of the legacy or entitlement. It is also important to note the principle established in *Kane v. Radley-Kane* [1999] Ch 274, namely that a sole executor may not appropriate an asset in favour of himself without the consent of the other beneficiaries.

If the beneficiary's consent is required for any appropriation, this can be achieved by an exchange of written correspondence and a note in the personal representative's records, which should include the beneficiary's instructions for the disposal of the asset. A convenient way to accomplish this is to complete a memorandum of appropriation, a specimen of which appears in **Appendix E**. It is possible to prepare one pro forma memorandum to cover a number of beneficiaries if necessary.

4.2.5 Appropriation of land to charity beneficiaries

If the personal representatives appropriate land to a charity beneficiary or beneficiaries and then sell that land as bare trustees, they will need to comply with the provisions of the Charities Act 2011, ss.117–123. This is because the property will be deemed to be 'charity land' and, among other requirements, a report from a qualified surveyor complying with the Charities Act 2011, s.119 must be obtained and considered prior to exchange of contracts. For more information, see *CC28 – Sales, Leases, Transfers or Mortgages: What Trustees Need to Know About Disposing of Charity Land* (Charity Commission, 2011).

It is important to note that ss.117–123 do not apply to a sale of land by personal representatives during the course of the administration, following an appropriation, where there are mixed (i.e. charitable and non-charitable) beneficiaries.

By contrast, however, these provisions do apply to a sale of land by trustees of a will trust, following the death of the life tenant, where only a charity or charities have a legal interest in the land. In that case, the trustees of the charity or charities which are the remainder beneficiaries will have to comply with these sections.

Trustees of exempt charities must fulfil their general duties when disposing of or mortgaging charity land. The restrictions contained in the Charities Act 2011, ss.117–123 do not apply to exempt charities. However, an exempt charity must include in the documentation relating to a disposition or mortgage the statements required by the Charities Act 2011, ss.122 and 125 respectively. For more information, see *CC23 – Exempt Charities* (Charity Commission, 2012).

4.3 Inheritance Tax (IHT)

All legacies to charities usually attract full IHT exemption (subject to **4.4** below). The exemption should be claimed on the IHT return submitted to HM Revenue and Customs when applying for the grant of representation.

By virtue of the Inheritance Tax Act (IHTA) 1984, s.41(b), any tax attributable to a non-exempt share of residue should be borne only by that share of residue. This can give rise to problems where a residuary estate is divided between exempt and non-exempt beneficiaries.

4.3.1 *Ratcliffe* or *Benham* construction

Personal representatives will need to consider how the estate is divided between the exempt and the non-exempt residuary beneficiaries. Do they receive an equal gross share in the estate (the gross approach) or do they receive an equal net share in the estate after the payment of IHT (the net approach)? This is important because the net approach results in a higher liability for IHT for the estate.

This area is governed by the landmark case *Re Ratcliffe (deceased)* (1999) STC 262, which followed an earlier decision.

Benham construction

The court had applied the net approach in *Re Benham's Will Trusts* (1995) STC 210, but the decision turned on the particular words used by the testatrix. This is different from the wording in most professionally drafted wills, which direct that estates should be divided after payment of debts and funeral and testamentary expenses (including IHT), but do not direct that the charities and non-charities should receive equal net amounts.

Ratcliffe construction

Ratcliffe established the principle that the gross approach should always be applied in estates that are divided between exempt and non-exempt beneficiaries, unless there is specific wording in the will to provide for a *Benham* division.

A common mistake is to deduct IHT from the residue before dividing it between the residuary beneficiaries. This has the effect of giving non-exempt beneficiaries the benefit of some of the exempt beneficiaries' status, and thus infringes the provision of IHTA 1984, s.41.

4.3.2 Grossing up

It does not always follow, however, that charitable residue will not bear any IHT. Where there are non-exempt legacies that exceed the nil-rate band, these will have to be grossed up for IHT purposes, and the tax borne by the residue equally (IHTA 1984, s.38). Similarly, when there are non-exempt pecuniary and/or specific gifts and the residue is partly exempt and partly non-exempt, double grossing up will need to be performed to calculate the IHT liability. The tax will then have to be apportioned between the whole of the residue (tax attributable to pecuniary and specific gifts) and the non-exempt residue (tax attributable to that part). The HM Revenue and Customs website includes a helpful grossing up calculator at www.hmrc.gov.uk/agents/iht/grossing-up-calcs.htm.

4.3.3 How to show the IHT liability in the estate accounts

The easiest way to show the IHT liability in the estate accounts is to include a schedule showing the calculations and apportionment. IHT can be deducted from the whole of the residue and the tax attributable to the non-exempt part added back in to the exempt part. Alternatively, the IHT attributable to the non-exempt share of residue should be deducted solely from that share.

Charity legacy professionals of larger charities are likely to have experience in the calculation of IHT in these types of estates, and may be willing to assist.

4.4 Finance Bill 2012 reduction of IHT rate

The Finance Bill 2012 provides for a reduction in the rate of IHT to be charged on transfers made on death that include gifts to charities (s.207 and Sched.32, which inserts a new Sched.1A into IHTA 1984).

The aim of the policy is to act as an incentive for people to make charitable legacies, or to increase existing legacies, and so increase the amount that charities receive from estates. A summary of these measures can be found on the HM Treasury website at www.hm-treasury.gov.uk/d/reduced_iht_charities.pdf.

4.4.1 Reduced rate of IHT

Under the new provisions, the rate of IHT will reduce from 40 per cent to 36 per cent where 10 per cent or more of a deceased person's net estate or component(s) of their net estate (after deducting IHT exemptions, reliefs and the nil-rate band) is left to charity. This legislation applies where the date of death is on or after 6 April 2012. It applies where the legacy is included in the will, but also where a will or the intestacy provisions have been varied by way of a deed of variation.

4.4.2 Components of an estate

For the purpose of this relief, the different components of an estate comprise the free estate (the 'general component'), assets owned jointly (the 'survivorship component'), and settled assets in which the deceased had a vested interest (the 'settled property component').

4.4.3 'Baseline amount'

The '10 per cent test', namely whether or not the 10 per cent threshold has been met, is determined by reference to the 'baseline amount', as set out in IHTA 1984, Sched.1A, para.5 (as inserted by the Finance Bill, Sched.32, para.1) for each of the three components. The baseline amount is determined as follows:

1. Calculate the value of the chargeable transfer attributable to the property in the component in question.
2. Deduct from that value the portion of the available nil-rate band attributable to that component.
3. Add an amount equal to the portion of the value transferred by the chargeable transfer which (in total) is attributable to property that forms part of that component (and is property in relation to which IHTA 1984, s.23(1) applies).

For each component, the 10 per cent test compares the baseline amount with the 'donated amount', which is the total value of assets given to charity which qualify for exemption under IHTA 1984.

4.4.4 Merging of components

Paragraph 7 of Sched.1A to IHTA 1984 (as inserted by the Finance Bill, Sched.32, para.1) allows the executors to elect for two or more components of the estate to be merged, where the amount given to charity from one or more components is at least 10 per cent of the baseline amount for that component. If the combined components pass the 10 per cent test, then they will be treated as a single component which will qualify for the 36 per cent rate. The election must be made in writing to HM Revenue and Customs within two years of death.

4.4.5 Notifying the charity of a deed of variation

Paragraph 9 of Sched.32 to the Finance Bill introduces amendments to IHTA 1984, s.142 so that where dispositions contained in a will are varied by deed of variation to include a gift to charity, such variation is not to be 'read back' into the will unless the people entering into the deed of variation demonstrate that the charity has been notified of the variation. These changes apply regardless of whether or not the variation allows the estate, or component(s) of the estate, to qualify for the reduced rate of tax.

4.4.6 Examples of the application of the lower 36 per cent IHT rate

The examples in the box below illustrate the IHT liability if 2 per cent, 4 per cent, 8 per cent, 10 per cent or 25 per cent of an estate passes to charity where the baseline amount is £1,000,000, all the assets are within the general component and there is no available nil-rate band.

Percentage passing to charity	2%	4%	8%	10%	25%
Amount passing to charity	20,000	40,000	80,000	100,000	250,000
Amount passing to non-charitable beneficiaries	588,000	576,000	552,000	576,000	480,000
IHT	392,000	384,000	368,000	324,000	270,000
Total (baseline amount)	1,000,000	1,000,000	1,000,000	1,000,000	1,000,000

The important point to note about the arithmetic in the above examples is that, in the cases where 4 per cent and 10 per cent passes to charity, the non-charitable beneficiaries receive exactly the same amount.

Another point to highlight is that, where 8 per cent passes to charity, the non-charitable beneficiaries actually receive a smaller amount because the rate of IHT in that case remains at 40 per cent.

See **Appendix F** for a draft model clause for wills published by the Society of Trust and Estate Practitioners (STEP) for use by individuals wishing to leave a legacy which will qualify under the new provisions.

4.5 Bodies that do not benefit from tax concessions

Only registered, exempt and excepted charities benefit from the tax concessions discussed in this chapter. Some organisations appear to be charitable in operation and objects, but in fact do not fulfil the criteria for the above classes of organisation. An example would be the National Anti-Vivisection Society. The status of all beneficiaries should be checked either directly with the organisation or with the Charity Commission. Some non-charitable organisations do, however, have associated charitable arms and it may therefore be possible to ensure that full exemptions are available to these bodies.

Chapter 5

Other issues affecting charities and estates

5.1 Charities as income beneficiaries

Very occasionally, a client names a charity to benefit from the income of an asset until the asset is redeemed or the trust otherwise falls-in. In such circumstances, the charity needs to have early information about the nature of the asset and its value. If the trust fund has arisen by virtue of an estate administration, then a copy of the estate accounts will be appreciated by the charity.

5.2 Discretionary legacies

When a will contains a wholly discretionary bequest, this will be notified to subscribing charities by Smee & Ford Ltd once the will has become public. While there is a danger of flooding executors and their representatives with appeals, many charities will wish to apply for discretionary funds as it is possible that their work could benefit substantially.

In many such cases, while the published will may appear wholly discretionary, the testator has either left a separate, private letter of wishes or otherwise communicated to their trustees their preferences for distribution.

5.3 Deeds of variation

Deeds of variation can be employed for a number of reasons. However, the most popular is to mitigate liability for IHT (IHTA 1984, s.142) and/or CGT (Taxation of Chargeable Gains Act 1992, s.62(6)). When there are two deaths in quick succession, it may be possible to vary the will (or wills) to ensure that the fullest use of any nil-rate bands is achieved.

> **Example A**
>
> Mr A dies and leaves an estate worth £1 million to his spouse, Mrs A. On Mrs A's death, she leaves her residue to their daughter, Mrs B. Although Mrs A's estate benefits from the transferable nil-rate band, the excess is still taxable for IHT purposes. Mrs B could vary the will of Mrs A so that, instead of inheriting the whole of Mrs A's estate, she only inherits up to the tax threshold, with the excess passing to charity. This would reduce the liability for IHT to zero.

Example B

Another opportunity to save IHT will occur on the successive deaths of two unmarried individuals. For example, Mr D dies leaving an estate worth £500,000 to Miss E, who dies shortly afterwards. Miss E has left her estate entirely to Charity Y. Mr D's will can be varied to omit the residuary gift to Miss E and replace it with a gift to Charity Y. Thus, a refund of the tax can be obtained.

It is important to note that any such deed of variation must be executed within two years of the date of death. However, it is no longer necessary to make an election to HM Revenue and Customs unless the variation alters the amount of IHT payable in the estate.

5.4 The transferable nil-rate band

The advent of the transferable nil-rate band (TNRB) occasionally leads to differences of opinion in assessing the value of legacies linked to the nil-rate band where residue passes to charity.

The beneficiaries of 'nil-rate band legacies' may hope that the value of their legacy will be topped up with the value of the TNRB. Charities taking the benefit of the residuary estate will be concerned to ensure that 'topping up' occurs only in instances where the wording clearly permits it.

HM Revenue and Customs previously issued helpful guidance on transferring an unused IHT threshold (**www.hmrc.gov.uk/inheritancetax/intro/transfer-threshold.htm**) which made it clear that where the legacy is defined by reference to the nil-rate band or the maximum available immediately before death it will not carry with it the benefit of the TNRB. Charities generally expect executors to adopt the same reasoning.

Appendix A

Example letter requesting a *Larke* v. *Nugus* statement

The following letter is reproduced with the kind permission of the Association of Contentious Trust and Probate Specialists (ACTAPS), www.actaps.com.

The letter makes reference to the Guide to the Professional Conduct of Solicitors 1999. Current professional rules are contained in the SRA Handbook *(Law Society, 2011; updated online at www.sra.org.uk) and good practice guidance on this topic is given in the Law Society's Practice Note: Disputed Wills (2011).*

Joint application letter to solicitors who prepared will requesting *Larke* v. *Nugus* statement

Dear Sirs

[*Name of deceased*] deceased

We, the undersigned Messrs [*firm's name*] [ref:] of [*firm's address*], solicitors for the Executors named in the Will of [*deceased's name*] of [*deceased's address*] and we, the undersigned Messrs [*firm's name*] [ref:] of [*firm's address*], solicitors for parties interested in his/her estate regret to inform you that [*deceased's name*] died on [*date of death*].

We understand that you drafted the deceased's last will dated [   ].

You may be aware that in 1959 the Law Society recommended that in circumstances such as this the testator's solicitor should make available a statement of his or her evidence regarding instructions for the preparation and execution of the will and surrounding circumstances. This recommendation was endorsed by the Court of Appeal on 21 February 1979 in *Larke* v. *Nugus*.

The practice is also recommended at paragraph 24.02 of the Law Society's Guide to the Professional Conduct of Solicitors, 7th edition (page 387).

Accordingly, we hereby request and authorise you to forward to each of the aforementioned firms statements from all appropriate members of your firm on the following points:

- How long had you known the deceased?
- Who introduced you to the deceased?
- On what date did you receive instructions from the deceased?
- Did you receive instructions by letter? If so, please provide copies of any correspondence.
- If instructions were taken at a meeting, please provide copies of your contemporaneous notes of the meeting including an indication of where the meeting took place and who else was present at the meeting.
- How were the instructions expressed?
- What indication did the deceased give to you that he knew he was making a will?
- Were you informed or otherwise aware of any medical history of the deceased that might bear upon the issue of his capacity?
- Did the deceased exhibit any signs of confusion or loss of memory? If so, please give details.

EXAMPLE LETTER REQUESTING A LARKE V. NUGUS STATEMENT

- To what extent were earlier wills discussed and what attempts were made to discuss departures from his earlier will-making pattern? What reasons, if any, did the testator give for making any such departures?
- When the will had been drafted, how were the provisions of the will explained to the deceased?
- Who, apart from the attesting witnesses, was present at the execution of the will? Where, when and how did this take place?
- Please provide copies of any other documents relating to your instructions for the preparation and execution of the will and surrounding circumstances or confirm that you have no objection to us inspecting your relevant file(s) on reasonable notice.

We confirm that we will be responsible for your reasonable photocopying charges in this connection and your invoice in this regard should be sent to [*each firm's name, etc.*] and marked for the attention of [*each firm's ref.*].

Dated this [ ] day of [   ] 20[ ]

Signed

……………………………………

Appendix B

Will clauses

B1 Pecuniary bequest

I give to Charity X of [*full address*] Charity Registration Number: [NNNNNNN] the sum of £_____ [*amount in words*] for its general purposes and I direct that the receipt of the Treasurer or other duly authorised officer shall be a sufficient discharge to my Executors.

B2 Specific bequest

I give to Charity X of [*full address*] Charity Registration Number: [NNNNNNN] [*description of item(s)*] absolutely for its general purposes and I direct that the receipt of the Treasurer or other duly authorised officer shall be a sufficient discharge to my Executors.

B3 Residuary bequest

I give to Charity X of [*full address*] Charity Registration Number: [NNNNNNN] [*proportion of residue*] for its general purposes and I direct that the receipt of the Treasurer or other duly authorised officer shall be a sufficient discharge to my Executors.

B4 Wording to express a testator's wish

... and I express the wish, but without creating any legally binding obligation, that the said charity use the said bequest for [*intended use*].

B5 Wording to appoint a charity as executor

I appoint Charity X of [*full address*] Charity Registration Number: [NNNNNNN] as Executor [*or* co-Executor] and Trustee of my estate.

B6 Wording for a bequest to a church

I give to the Vicar and Churchwardens of X Church of [*full address*] the sum of £_____ [*amount in words*]/[*proportion of residue*]/[*description of specific item*] for its general purposes and I direct that the receipt of the Treasurer or other duly authorised officer shall be a sufficient discharge to my Executors.

B7 General cy-près clause

If before my death (or after my death but before my trustees have given effect to the gift), any charitable or other body to which a gift is made by this will or any codicil to it has changed its name or amalgamated with any other body, or transferred all its assets to any other body, then my trustees shall give effect to the gift as if it were a gift to the body in its changed name or to the body resulting from the amalgamation or to the body to which the assets have been transferred.

Appendix C

Sample Smee & Ford notification

Smee & Ford Ltd Week ending: 27/04/2012

REPORT OF A CHARITABLE BEQUEST

The Will of Mr Some Body,
of The Gate House, SomeTown, AB1 2CD

dated 19/01/2007,
contains the following bequests, subject to payment of other legacies, debts and testamentary expenses:

£5,000 to Age Concern, SomeTown Centre

£5,000 to Friends of Royal Victoria Hospital (with the wish that it be used in the Children's Unit)

and

1/3rd of the residue each to:

The British Heart Foundation

Save the Children UK

(balance to personal legatees)

The testator died on: 19/02/2012

leaving:
gross estate valued at £1,148,924
net estate valued at £1,147,074

The Will was proved at the LEEDS Probate Registry of the Family Division on 15/03/2012
Executors: Some One of 175 Example Street, SomeTown, WX1 2YZ and Another One of 125 Example Street, SomeTown, WX1 2YZ.
Extracting solicitors: Smith, Smith & Jones of 150 Example Street, SomeTown, WX1 2YZ

This notice merely indicates that a charity is mentioned in the above will. It does not imply that rights to benefit exist, as prior rights may not be known. The amount of the estate available for distribution does not necessarily correspond with the net value of the estate given above.

Appendix D

Royal Sign Manual directions

The following article by Victoria Forwood was previously published in the ILM Newsletter *and is reproduced here with the kind permission of the Institute of Legacy Management. At the time of writing the article, Victoria was a barrister in the charities team of the Treasury Solicitor's Department.*

If the reader recalls nothing else from this article, he or she is invited to remember just two things:

1. There is no charity called 'Cancer Research'; and
2. When drawing up a will, solicitors should check that the charity or charities named actually exist.

In most cases this can be done by checking the Register of Charities on the Charity Commission's web site (**www.charitycommission.gov.uk**) or by a telephone call either to the Commission or to the charity in question. Where a charity has changed its name, both the former and current name may be listed in the Institute of Legacy Management database; contact ILM via **www.legacymanagement.org.uk**.

Regrettably, and all too frequently, this simple check is not done and personal representatives are left with the problem of disposing of direct gifts to non-existent charities or for charitable purposes where no particular charity or trustee has been selected by the testator. This problem is hardly novel, but it may surprise some to learn that there exists under our unwritten constitution a little known and possibly anachronistic prerogative power whose existence can be traced back to the seventeenth century and beyond, which provides us in the twenty first century with a quick and cost effective procedure to resolve it. That procedure is a direction from the Attorney General under the Royal Sign Manual.

What is the Royal Sign Manual?

The Royal Sign Manual is, literally, the signature of the monarch. Directions disposing of charitable gifts were signed by the Queen until 3 May 1986, when she delegated her power to dispose of charitable gifts to the Attorney General. Since section 1 of the Law Officers Act 1997 came into force directions can also be signed by the Solicitor General.

What does a Sign Manual direction do?

It identifies the charitable beneficiary whose identity was previously uncertain. The jurisdiction is analogous to that of the court and the Charity Commissioners to make administrative schemes in respect of charitable gifts. The personal representatives must then administer the gift in accordance with the direction.

When is it used?

It is used for giving effect to direct gifts for charitable purposes when no particular objects or trustees have been selected by a testator. These gifts can either be gifts for charitable purposes expressed in general terms or the testator could have named what appears at first blush to be an organisation with charitable objects but, on further investigation, none is found to exist with that name.

Frequently encountered examples of the first type are gifts in wills to 'cancer research', 'arthritis research', 'kidney research' and the like. Less common examples include gifts for 'research into a cure for herpes zoster', 'handicapped children', 'churches', 'conservation', 'animal welfare', 'a charity for the care of donkeys' and 'to charity'.

Examples of gifts to organisations with charitable objects that never existed include gifts to 'The Hospital for Incurable Women of Brompton Road, London', 'Save the Horses Fund', 'the Ethiopia Fund', 'the Cancer Research Trust', 'the London Preservation Society' and 'the association for the preservation of tropical rainforests'.

When is it not used?

- It cannot be used to construe a will. If by construing the will as a whole a charity can be identified, then the personal representatives can pay the legacy to that charity without the need for a direction. For example, a gift to 'cancer research' followed by the address of Macmillan Cancer Support is capable of being construed as a gift to Macmillan Cancer Support.
- It cannot be used to resolve a dispute over the validity or construction of a will. The Attorney General will generally not make a direction if he is aware that there is or may be a dispute pending.
- It does not protect personal representatives from challenge from persons claiming to be beneficially entitled to the gift in question.
- It cannot be used by the Attorney General for England and Wales in relation to Scottish or Northern Irish estates in respect of which there are probably no analogous powers.
- It cannot be used when a trust has been interposed on the gift. The jurisdiction was analysed by Mr Justice Vaisey in *Re Bennett deceased* [1960] Ch 18, who commented at page 24:

  > It is a curious thing that the matter seems on the authorities to depend almost entirely on this principle: was the gift to the non-existent beneficiary created by means of a trust or by a direct gift? If it was created by means of a trust, then the usual procedure would follow, and it would be for the court to decide, in the familiar way, by way of scheme what should be done with the disputed amount. If, on the other hand, the gift to the non-existent hospital is not by way of trust but a direct gift, then under a very long series of authorities (not altogether consistent and not altogether easy to interpret) it falls to be dealt with by the royal prerogative.

- It is not used where the testator has provided in his or her will for the eventuality of an organisation with charitable objects named in his will not existing and provides for his personal representatives to decide which charity should benefit from the gift.

Since when has it been used?

Its use can be traced back to at least 1675. In *AG v. Peacock* (1675) Finch 245, Lord Nottingham LC upheld a bequest 'to charitable uses for the good of the poor for ever' on the ground that 'the King by his prerogative could cure the uncertainty and apply the property cy-près to like charitable objects under the sign manual'. Charles II, who was known to be interested in the welfare of social and educational charities, directed that the money be applied for the benefit of the poor children of his new royal foundation in Christ's Hospital who were to be taught arithmetic and the art of navigation.

How is a charity selected by the Attorney General?

In determining how to dispose of the gift the Attorney General adopts the same approach as would be adopted by the court. The factors to which he will have regard are:

- The testator's intentions as expressed in his or her will: a gift to 'asthma research' will be applied to a charity which conducts research into asthma;
- Extrinsic evidence that suggests the testator had a particular charity in mind when he or she made the will; for example, sometimes there will be a record of a testator donating to a particular charity during his or her lifetime; sometimes the testator is known to have supported a local charity shop; sometimes it can be established that the testator pledged a legacy to a particular charity; and sometimes the testator may have made known the wishes to his or her executors, family or friends.

The Attorney General will then consider all the evidence, and a direction will normally be made in accordance with the testator's perceived intentions, although the Attorney General is not bound by these.

What is the Treasury Solicitor's procedure?

The Treasury Solicitor acts for the Attorney General in these cases, and is the person to whom requests should be directed in the first instance.

- When personal representatives or their solicitors first make contact, they are provided with a copy of a note of procedure and asked for (a) sight of the original grant of probate or letters of administration with will annexed, (b) any other evidence as to the charity the testator intended to benefit and (c) the value of the gift where this is not apparent from the will.
- The Treasury Solicitor will then check the Register of Charities both to check that no charity exists with that name and identify charities that further the purposes the testator intended to benefit.
- When enquiries are complete, a submission and draft direction will be put up to either the Attorney General or Solicitor General for his or her consideration.
- The signed direction is generally returned to the Treasury Solicitor within a few days.
- The original direction is then forwarded to the personal representatives.

Some facts and figures

The Attorney General is currently making approximately 50 Sign Manual directions a year. Most of these bequests are small (£1,000 or less). By far, the most common use for directions is in respect of gifts to 'cancer research'. A significant proportion of wills are 'homemade'.

The cancer research rota

Because by far the largest number of cases referred to the Attorney General for a direction concern gifts to 'cancer research' and because there will often be no evidence that the testator had a particular cancer research charity in mind, a system has been developed whereby such gifts are applied in accordance with a 'rota'. There are currently seven charities that conduct research into cancer on the rota: Cancer Research UK, The Institute of Cancer Research, The Leukaemia Research Fund, Breakthrough Breast Cancer, Tenovus, The Roy Castle Lung Cancer Foundation and Marie Curie Cancer Care. Although called a rota, it is not a true rota. Instead, each gift is applied to the charity with the lowest running total so that each receives roughly equal amounts over a period of time. Very large gifts may be shared equally between all seven rota charities. The amount distributed under the rota can vary substantially from year to year but is roughly £800,000 per annum.

Advantages

A direction under the Royal Sign Manual procedure has two notable advantages: it is cheap, and it is quick. The Attorney General does not charge for a direction; when solicitors or banks administering the estate drafted the will in question, they are requested not to charge for their time in procuring a direction. Except in cases where there is a dispute, a direction can usually be made within weeks.

In exceptional cases (for example, when the person entitled to take out the grant under rule 20 of the Non Contentious Probate Rules 1987 is the residuary beneficiary and a direction is required to ascertain the identity of that beneficiary) directions will be made before a grant of probate or letters of administration with will annexed have been extracted.

Personal representatives or their solicitors who would like the Attorney General to make a direction in a particular case should write to the charities team of the Treasury Solicitor's Department, 1 Kemble Street, London WC2B 4TS.

Appendix E

Memorandum of appropriation for investments

Specimen memorandum of appropriation

Miss A N Other deceased

1. Miss Alicia Nora Other (The Testatrix) late of Example Street, Some Town, WX1 2YZ, died on 1 August 2011.
2. The Will dated 1 January 1998 was proved by Some One and Another One at the Leeds Probate Registry on 1 October 2011.
3. Under the terms of the Will, the ABC Charity of 1 Any Street, Any Town, WX1 2YZ is entitled to a one-third share of the residuary estate.
4. The stocks and shares set out in the Schedule hereto are no longer required in the administration of the estate.

We, Some One and Another One, as Personal Representatives of Alicia Nora Other hereby give notice to ABC Charity that we have today together appropriated the stocks and shares set out in the Schedule hereto in part satisfaction of the said Charity's one-third share of the residuary estate of the Testatrix.

As from the date hereof, we the Executors declare that we shall hold the shares set out in the Schedule hereto as 'bare' Trustees for ABC Charity and not as Personal Representatives of Alicia Nora Other.

Suggested format for a schedule of stocks and shares appropriated to ABC Charity and referred to above

Name of company	Number of shares appropriated (i.e. ABC Charity share)

Dated this [.......] day of [..........] 20[...]

Signed by:

Some One   Another One

We hereby acknowledge that we have received a Notice of which the above is a duplicate.

Signed: Date:

For and on behalf of ABC Charity

Appendix F

STEP draft model clause for wills benefitting a charity to satisfy the 10 per cent test

The Society of Trust and Estate Practitioners (STEP) has published a draft model clause for wills in response to the Finance Bill 2012 which proposes a reduced rate of Inheritance Tax (IHT) where there is a charitable legacy of 10 per cent or more left in a will.

*The proposed model clause allows people to set aside assets from their estate for the purpose of charitable giving. The model clause is currently in draft and will be reviewed when the final wording of the legislation is known (see **www.step.org**).*

The text reproduced below is an extract from STEP's submission to HM Revenue and Customs containing the draft clause and comments from STEP.

Draft clause

We set out in the Appendix to our previous submission a possible model clause that might be adopted by persons wishing to leave a legacy qualifying for the new relief.

The draft clause requires amendment so as to be consistent with the definitions and structure provided in Schedule 1A. We had considered amending the clause also to encompass the possibility of the legacy being varied under a formula should an election be made for another component to be treated as a single component with the free estate by an election under paragraph 7.

On reflection we have not included such an amendment. This is for two reasons.

Firstly, complexity. Further, in many cases such a provision will not be needed. Such a clause could be drafted on a bespoke basis if it were needed and thought to be possible. Secondly, questions of an unauthorised delegation of testamentary authority might arise because the deceased may be seen to have delegated to others the ability to vary the value of the legacies to charity by making or omitting to make an election under paragraph 7.

We have however included the more limited option of leaving a legacy of 10 per cent or more of an aggregate of the general and other components irrespective of whether an election under paragraph 7 is made. It would then be for the relevant persons to decide whether or not to make an election under paragraph 7 but in doing so they would not alter the size of the legacy. This does not give rise to the concerns mentioned in the previous paragraph.

Appendix

We set out below a possible model clause that might be adopted by persons wishing to leave a legacy qualifying for the new relief.

It would be most helpful to practitioners and taxpayers generally if HMRC would confirm that such a clause (with any appropriate amendments) would be accepted as complying with the requirements of Schedule 1A.

Any clause of a general nature like this would need to be qualified to deal with the concerns set out below.

The first such concern is that a legacy defined by reference to the relief will fail if the estate turns out to be below the threshold for a taxable estate: if there were no TP within paragraph 1(2). Another concern is that a legacy drafted so as to qualify for relief might leave to charity too much as a proportion of the estate passing on the death of the testator. This might arise, for example, if the estate on the death was worth less than anticipated. In such a case there might be a risk that the dependants of the deceased would be prejudiced.

The clause below is designed to provide for a legacy which would qualify for relief but which also contains optional provisos designed to address the concerns mentioned above.

Proviso (ii) addresses the second concern referred to above that the legacy to charity might comprise too large a proportion of the estate on death. The consequence of including the proviso may be that 10 per cent threshold is not met and that relief would not be available subject to a possible election under paragraph 7 if there was another component which was a qualifying component. The proviso includes a number of options. In the event that the proviso is included the testator or testatrix may wish to alter the amount of the legacy or indeed to omit it entirely should the proviso apply. The appropriate option could be adopted.

We have in addition included administrative provisions which while not essential to the clause being effective in attracting relief under Schedule 1A would nonetheless be useful to executors.

Draft clause

1.1 I give [*name of charity*] such a sum as shall constitute a donated amount equal to 10 [*or insert larger figure*] per cent (%) of the baseline amount in relation to the [general component] [aggregate of the general, [survivorship] and [settled property] components] of my estate.

1.2 [The legacy given by this clause shall in no event:
   1.2.1 be less than £[ ] whether or not the lower rate of tax shall be applicable; and
   1.2.2 exceed £[ ] (the upper limit) even if in consequence of this restriction in the value of this legacy the lower rate of tax shall not apply. [If this proviso shall apply and in consequence the lower rate of tax shall not be payable the amount of this legacy shall [be equal to the amount of the upper limit] [be reduced to £[ ]] [lapse].]

1.3 My executors in making payment of the legacy given by this clause:
   1.3.1 shall be entitled to accept in full discharge the receipt of the secretary, treasurer or other officer of the charity concerned;
   1.3.2 may appropriate assets not otherwise specifically bequeathed to satisfy (or partly satisfy) this legacy without the consent of any beneficiary under my will or any codicil to my will.

1.4 I hereby confer on my executors the power to make or withdraw any of the following elections:

    1.4.1 an election under paragraph 7 whether or not the general component is the qualifying component; and

    1.4.2 an election under paragraph 8.

1.5 For the purposes of this clause 'baseline amount', 'donated amount', 'general component', 'lower rate of tax', 'qualifying component', 'settled property component' and 'survivorship component' shall have the meanings they respectively bear in Schedule 1A to the Inheritance Tax Act 1984 and references to paragraph numbers concerning the making or withdrawing of an election are to the paragraphs bearing the same number in Schedule 1A to that Act.

Appendix G

Further reading

ACTAPS Practice Guidance Notes for the Resolution of Trust and Probate Disputes (ACTAPS Code) (Association of Contentious Trust and Probate Specialists, 2006)

Appointment of a Professional Executor Practice Note (Law Society, 2011)

CC7 – *Ex Gratia Payments by Charities* (Charity Commission, 2001)

CC23 – *Exempt Charities* (Charity Commission, 2012)

CC28 – *Sales, Leases, Transfers or Mortgages: What Trustees Need to Know About Disposing of Charity Land* (Charity Commission, 2011)

Disputed Wills Practice Note (Law Society, 2011)

File Retention: Will and Probate Practice Note (Law Society, 2011)

Legacy Fundraising Code of Fundraising Practice (Institute of Fundraising, 2007)

Mental Capacity Act 2005: Code of Practice (Department for Constitutional Affairs, 2007)

Non-Contentious Costs (Law Society, 2011)

OG11 – *Operational Guidance: Ex Gratia Payments by Charities* (Charity Commission)

Paying for Wills with Charity Funds (Charity Commission)

Probate Practitioner's Handbook, 6th edition (Law Society, 2011)

SRA Handbook 2011 (Law Society, 2011) (3rd edition published online at **www.sra.org.uk**)

Will Draftsman's Handbook, 9th edition (Law Society, 2012)

Appendix H
Useful links

Association of Contentious Trust and Probate Specialists
www.actaps.com

Attorney General's Office
www.attorneygeneral.gov.uk

Charities Aid Foundation
www.cafonline.org

Charity Choice
www.charitychoice.co.uk

Charities Commission
www.charity-commission.gov.uk

Court of Protection
www.justice.gov.uk/courts/rcj-rolls-building/court-of-protection#

HM Revenue and Customs
www.hmrc.gov.uk

Institute of Fundraising
www.institute-of-fundraising.org.uk

Law Society of England and Wales
www.lawsociety.org.uk

Law Society Gazette
www.lawgazette.co.uk

Law Society Gazette Charity Explorer
www.lawgazette.co.uk/charityexplorer

Law Society's Private Client Section
www.probatesection.org.uk

Remember a Charity Campaign
www.rememberacharity.org.uk

Smee & Ford Ltd
www.smeeandford.co.uk

Solicitors Regulation Authority
www.sra.org.uk

USEFUL LINKS

Society of Trust and Estate Practitioners (STEP)
www.step.org

Treasury Solicitor
www.tsol.gov.uk

Will Aid
www.willaid.org.uk